My
School Days Memory
Book
for
Grade:

A Picture of Me on the First Day of School

When I Grow Up I want to Be A:

Notes

Name:

Date:

School:

Principal:

Teacher(s)

Other School Staff That I Know:

Notes

September

A September Picture

There are _____Kids in My Class

Girls:_____   Boys:_____

Kids I Know in My Class Already

New Friends I've Made

My Best Friends Are:

Who I Like to Eat My Lunch With:

My Favorite Thing To Take in My Lunch Is:

My Favorite Thing to Do at Recess Is:

My Favorite Thing About September

The Funniest Thing That Happened This Month:

The Scariest Thing That Happened This Month:

The Happiest Thing That Happened This Month:

What I Was Most Proud of This Month:

Notes

October

An October Picture

Who I Like to Eat My Lunch With:

My Favorite Thing To Take in My Lunch Is:

My Favorite Thing to Do at Recess Is:

My Favorite Thing About October:

The Funniest Thing That Happened This Month:

The Scariest Thing That Happened This Month:

The Happiest Thing That Happened This Month:

What I Was Most Proud of This Month:

For Halloween I was a:

My Halloween Picture

Notes

November

A November Picture

The Funniest Thing That Happened This Month:

The Scariest Thing That Happened This Month:

The Happiest Thing That Happened This Month:

What I Was Most Proud of This Month:

Who I Like to Eat My Lunch With:

My Favorite Thing To Take in My Lunch Is:

My Favorite Thing to Do at Recess Is:

My Favorite Thing About November:

Notes

Notes

December

A December Picture

The Funniest Thing That Happened This Month:

The Scariest Thing That Happened This Month:

The Happiest Thing That Happened This Month:

What I Was Most Proud of This Month:

Who I Like to Eat My Lunch With:

My Favorite Thing To Take in My Lunch Is:

My Favorite Thing to Do at Recess Is:

My Favorite Thing About December:

For Christmas I Gave My Teacher A:

The Best Gift I Gave Someone Was::

The Best Gift I Received Was:

My Favorite Thing About Christmas Is:

Notes

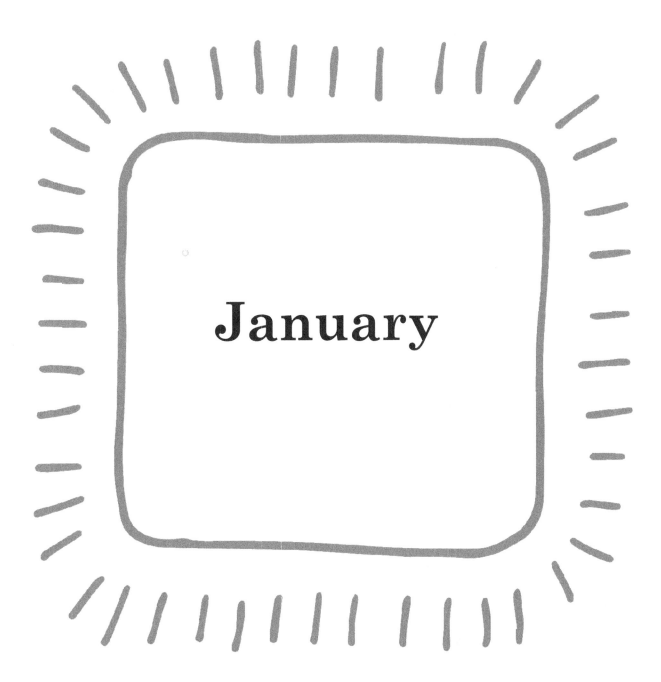

January

A January Picture

My New Year Resolutions For School Are:

My New Year Resolutions For Home Are:

The Funniest Thing That Happened This Month:

The Scariest Thing That Happened This Month:

The Happiest Thing That Happened This Month:

What I Was Most Proud of This Month:

Who I Like to Eat My Lunch With:

My Favorite Thing To Take in My Lunch Is:

My Favorite Thing to Do at Recess Is:

My Favorite Thing About January:

Notes

February

A February Picture

The Funniest Thing That Happened This Month:

The Scariest Thing That Happened This Month:

The Happiest Thing That Happened This Month:

What I Was Most Proud of This Month:

Who I Like to Eat My Lunch With:

My Favorite Thing To Take in My Lunch Is:

My Favorite Thing to Do at Recess Is:

My Favorite Thing About February:

How we celebrated Valentine's Day at School:

How we celebrated Valentine's Day at Home:

Notes

March

A March Picture

The Funniest Thing That Happened This Month:

The Scariest Thing That Happened This Month:

The Happiest Thing That Happened This Month:

What I Was Most Proud of This Month:

Who I Like to Eat My Lunch With:

My Favorite Thing To Take in My Lunch Is:

My Favorite Thing to Do at Recess Is:

My Favorite Thing About March:

Notes

Notes

April

An April Picture

The Funniest Thing That Happened This Month:

The Scariest Thing That Happened This Month:

The Happiest Thing That Happened This Month:

What I Was Most Proud of This Month:

Who I Like to Eat My Lunch With:

My Favorite Thing To Take in My Lunch Is:

My Favorite Thing to Do at Recess Is:

My Favorite Thing About April:

Notes

Notes

May

A May Picture

The Funniest Thing That Happened This Month:

The Scariest Thing That Happened This Month:

The Happiest Thing That Happened This Month:

What I Was Most Proud of This Month:

Who I Like to Eat My Lunch With:

My Favorite Thing To Take in My Lunch Is:

My Favorite Thing to Do at Recess Is:

My Favorite Thing About May:

Notes

Notes

June

A June Picture

The Funniest Thing That Happened This Month:

The Scariest Thing That Happened This Month:

The Happiest Thing That Happened This Month:

What I Was Most Proud of This Month:

Who I Like to Eat My Lunch With:

My Favorite Thing To Take in My Lunch Is:

My Favorite Thing to Do at Recess Is:

My Favorite Thing About June:

My Favorite Memory from This Year:

My Best Friends from This Year:

Things I Want to Do This Summer

Notes

Notes

July

A July Picture

I had the most fun this month when:

My Favorite Memory of July:

Notes

August

An August Picture

I had the most fun this month when:

My Favorite Memory of August:

My Best Summer Memory:

My Goals for Next Year at School:

Summer Doodles

Summer Doodles

Notes

Summer Doodles

Notes

Summer Doodles

Notes

Summer Doodles

Notes

Summer Doodles

Notes

Summer Doodles

Notes

Summer Doodles

Made in United States
North Haven, CT
20 May 2022